DEMOCRACY AND THE ARTS

DEMOCRACY
AND THE ARTS

Rupert Brooke

WITH A PREFACE BY
GEOFFREY KEYNES

London
RUPERT HART-DAVIS
1946

FIRST PUBLISHED 1946

PRINTED IN ENGLAND
BY WILLIAM CLOWES AND SONS, LIMITED
BOUND BY THE LEIGHTON-STRAKER BOOKBINDING COMPANY

PREFACE

RUPERT BROOKE went up to King's College, Cambridge, as an undergraduate in October, 1906. The political influences of his home life at Rugby had been strongly Liberal, but soon after arriving at Cambridge he began to show a tendency to move towards the Left. An early friend at King's was Hugh Dalton, now Chancellor of the Exchequer in the Labour Government. Dalton was then Honorary Secretary of the Cambridge University Fabian Society, and he has recorded [1] that in April, 1907, Brooke came to him and said, "I'm not your sort of Socialist; I'm a William Morris sort of Socialist, but I want to join your Society as an Associate". According to Dalton, he soon saw the intellectual limitations of a "William Morris sort of Socialist" and then became a full member of the Fabian Society. For the academic year 1909–1910 he was elected President. Meetings were sometimes held in Brooke's rooms in King's, where, as J. T. Sheppard, now Provost of the College, recalls, the Fabians would be entertained to a frugal repast of bread and cheese and beer. At these meetings he was never tired of teaching the importance of poets and artists in the good society of the future, and Dalton has also testified that " he came to talk very good sense on the larger economic questions".

It was probably during his Presidency of the

[1] In the *Memoir* by Sir Edward Marsh first published with the *Collected Poems* in 1918.

C.U.F.S., in the spring or summer of 1910, that Brooke read his paper to the Fabians entitled "Democracy and the Arts". I was myself present at the meeting as an Associate Member, though I cannot now remember any details of the occasion. I fear that I had joined the Society rather to please my friend than because of any deep political convictions, but I felt rewarded by having the stimulus and enjoyment of listening to speakers such as Bernard Shaw and, on more than one occasion, Brooke himself. The meeting is likely to have been in Brooke's rooms in Gibb's Buildings in the south-west corner of the first court of King's, and the speaker must have looked exactly as he appears in the portrait-study reproduced here from a photograph taken in 1910 by a Fellow of Trinity, V. H. Mottram.[1] Brooke was very much in earnest over his Socialism at this time, and even more in earnest in his solicitude for the Arts, particularly the art of poetry. By 1910 he had already been taking himself seriously as a poet for six or seven years, and his first volume of poetry was to appear in the next year, 1911. But in the early part of 1910 the endowment of Artists by a Socialist Government must have seemed a remote Utopian ideal, important indeed while engaging our attention through the vivid personality of our President, but only to be quickly forgotten when the evening's discussion was over with the disappearance of the bread and cheese and beer.

A few years after Brooke's death in 1915 his

[1] Late Professor of Physiology in the University of London.

PREFACE

mother gave me the manuscript of "Democracy and the Arts" during one of my periodical visits to her house at Rugby, and for nearly twenty-five years it has lain more or less unregarded in my library. Now, in 1946, the subject of the paper has suddenly become topical, more topical than when it was written, with the dawning of the Socialist State in England of which Brooke was one of the Minor Prophets. It has, therefore, seemed to me to be my duty [1] to present his paper for publication in print, since the claims of the Arts can so easily be overlooked among the many more material and pressing problems. Were he still alive, none would now be more eager to serve the Arts than Rupert Brooke, and it is therefore right to allow his voice, which will still be heard with respect, to speak to a wider public than the long-vanished gathering of young intellectuals who listened to him in his college rooms.

But his reputation as a poet and a writer must not arouse expectations of a polished literary composition in the pages that follow. It is obvious from the appearance of the pencilled manuscript that it was dashed off at a great speed, and it was read with but little revision. It is brusque and colloquial in style, with none of the literary graces of which the writer was capable. It was meant to be an example of what the Poet could do when he turned practical, and its value lies in the sincerity of the convictions which informed his mind, and the urgency with which he

[1] With the concurrence of Brooke's other Literary Trustees, Walter de la Mare, the Provost of King's and Dudley Ward.

vii

could present his case even when there was no immediate prospect of a system of society likely to be willing to carry it into effect. Even under a Coalition Government, and in conditions of war, a beginning was made in the recognition of the Arts by the official institution of C.E.M.A., now known as The Arts Council. Perhaps Brooke's words will remind the present Chancellor of the Exchequer (who may, indeed, never have forgotten) that once he too believed in the importance of the Arts in the national life, and he may be encouraged to assign to this object the funds that could do so much, if applied in the right way, to encourage the artists and to foster appreciation of their arts.

GEOFFREY KEYNES

May, 1946

DEMOCRACY AND THE ARTS

I AM NOT going to rhapsodize about the Spirit of Democracy as dawning in the operas of Wagner or the anarchic prose of Whitman or Carpenter. "Brotherhood" will not be heard of in this paper. Neither comrade nor cumrade shall be mentioned by me. I would detain you this side of the millennium. What I want to discuss, to ask one or two questions about, is the effect that a democratic form of society—*our* democratic form of society—has, and will have, on the production of pictures, music and literature; and how we are to control that effect. I nearly wrote a paper on "The Artist under Socialism", but I didn't for two reasons. One was that the phrase "under Socialism" regrettably tends to drop the pink gauze of unreality over the whole issue. The other was that I wanted not to scare off any good people, who, though Progressive, Democratic, Socialistic and the rest, can't bring themselves to be so absolutely sure as to call themselves *Socialists*, [or to believe] that the pearl-button industry really *ought* to be taken over by the State— at any rate just *yet*.

I use the word "Democracy". It seems to me that this century is going to witness a struggle between Democracy and Plutocracy. Democracy is the ordering of the national life according to the national will. Its probable and desirable increase in the near future entails a great growth in collective control, in various ways, of every side of the life of the nation, and

B

organizing—or wilfully not organizing—it to attain the collectively-willed good. It is not the time now to spread into how this growth of Democracy will insist on a great liberty and security and independence for each man. I feel sure that in this general question most people, in theory anyhow, will agree with me. And in the end it is one of the few questions that matter. I am one of those who care for the *result* of actions. If anybody tells me that an absolute hereditary monarchy based on slave labour, or an agricultural oligarchy of Plato's φύλακες, is the ideal state which *he* will always advocate, I can only take him up to a high place, and say, "My dear creature, up North there are twenty millions who want Democracy; down South there are twenty millions who want Plutocracy. Are you coming North with me?" And the same to any Democrat who tries to differ with me about, say, the exact relations between Local and National Government fifty years on.

This democratization of our land, then, which we so greatly desire (and which will require, I believe, so much Collectivism), will reduce the number of those who live on money they do not earn most or all their lives. Observe the situation, and remember it's a real one, not one in a book. (1) Art is important. (2) The people who produce art at present are, if you look into it, nearly always dependent on unearned income. (3) We are going to diminish and extinguish the number of those dependent on unearned income. We shall also reduce the number of those rich enough to act the patron to artists, and change in a thousand

other ways the circumstances of the arts and of the
artists.

We must, then, acknowledge that there may be
something in the objections of the average anti-
democrat, the refined vague upper-class person, that
we are making the arts impossible. The literature of
the future will be blue-books, its art framed plans of
garden cities. The anti-democrat himself is generally
easy enough to answer. The decay of Culture, he
wails, the neglect of Art, the absence of fine literature
—points to the halfpenny papers, shudders at the
grimy Philistines. You ask him how often *he* goes to
the National Gallery, how lately *he* has read the six
best plays of Shakespeare. . . . But the fact remains.
Very little attention is paid, as we change the struc-
ture of Society, to the claims of the Arts. Artists have
lived, in the past and present, on inherited capital
or on the patronage of rich men or corporations.
How are *we* going to arrange for them? I sympathize
—slightly—with those who airily cry, with Whistler,
"Art? Oh, Art—*happens!*" But that won't do. It
never would, or should, have done. Now least of
all. For while everything has, in a way, "happened"
hitherto, *now* we are trying this tremendous experi-
ment of Democracy, of taking our own fate into our
own hands, controlling the future, shaping Life to
our will. Now most of all when we are, however
roughly, trying to foresee and provide for everything, we must provide for Art. It is permissible to
take what flowers you find best in a wood. A garden
requires planning.

I've indicated what I mean by Democracy. I suppose the Arts don't need definition. Both these things will become clearer in the course of the paper. We want to see how we can produce as large and appreciative a public as possible; a state of things where the fineness (not the refinedness) of Art will enter deeply into many men's lives, and as many good works of art as possible. It is this last thing I am most concerned with, dealing with the producers and production, not the questions of distribution or consumption.

But it may be useful to discuss what we mean by Art a little further. The air is full of sentimentalities and false notions about it, and should be cleared. A good many people—especially democratic people—will say the question of Art and Artists has already been answered, and point to William Morris and the Arts and Crafts. This is very dangerous. There are several perils connected with that sort of thing. No answer to the question of Artists has come from these sources; not even a realization of the question. I want to disavow almost altogether what Mr. H. G. Wells once called Hampstead-and-Hammered-Copper Socialism (that was before he went to live at Hampstead). For one thing you must separate the questions of Art and of Crafts. *Crafts* I won't discuss now, beyond suggesting that you can't get a revival of Crafts by any movement consisting of people making a piece of unpolished furniture a year and living on dividends, and of bookbinding by unoccupied young ladies. It must come, if at all, through the Trades Unions. And anyhow, don't mix up Art and Crafts.

It is so easy to do so, and so tempting to slide from the keen edge of Art into the byways, the pursuits that don't disturb, the paths that lead to antiquarianism and hobbies, bibliography, love of seventeenth-century prose which is quaint, beautiful handwriting. These things are excellent, but not to the point. Revive handicrafts as much as you can for the sake of the Craftsman. Art is a different matter. We want *King Lear* and " The Polish Rider " for what we get out of them, not the pleasure it gives Shakespeare and Rembrandt to make them. Morris, or at least the Morrisite, approaches the matter from a wrong side. It is no good going back to the Middle Ages and the great communal art of the Cathedrals and the folk-songs. If you can revive communal art, well and good. But it is a small thing. We have done much better since. Individuals have made tunes and poems as good as those we are told came from the people. Burns, perhaps, has done so. And you won't find any band of mediæval rustics in an inn inspired to troll out *Paradise Lost* or a Beethoven Concerto between the bouts of mead.

We live in our own age (a very intelligent and vital one) and we must throw ourselves in with all its arts and schools of art, music, and literature. Tapestries are both unhealthy and ugly. Let romaunt and clavicithern moulder together.

But there arises from *dicta* of Morris a belief that too many hold—that art is an easy thing, a πάρεργον. Morris said, I believe, that all poetry ought to be of the kind a man can make up while he is working at a loom. Much of his own was. That may be why a lot of it is so dull. "Easy writing", someone said, "makes damned hard reading". Not so did Shakespeare or Balzac write or Beethoven compose. It is an infamous heresy of his, and it extends to other arts besides poetry, though it is about poetry most people hold it. It leads to this too common idea that the various artists of the future will be able to do ordinary work for so many hours a day, and pursue their arts in their leisure time. You don't find artists advocating that: only some of the ordinary cultured public. It is a thing we can't allow. It means the death of the Arts, a civilization of amiable amateurs, of intermittent Alexandrians. We have too much of this system already—it is no fault of the individual—the Civil Service poets, the stockbroker who does watercolours in the evenings, the music-master who has the holidays to compose in. Better, almost, a literature of blue-books than a literature of belles-lettres.

There is another wrong notion of art that falsifies the opinions of many on this subject. Let us beware of those who talk of "the art of the people", or of "expressing the soul of the Community". The Community hasn't got a soul; you can't voice the soul of the Community any more than you can blow its nose. The conditions of Democracy may profoundly alter the outlook of many artists, and partly their style and subject matter. But the *main* business of art has been, is, and, one must assume, will be an individual and unique affair. "I saw—*I* saw", the artist says, "a tree against the sky, or a blank wall in the sunlight, and it was so thrilling, so arresting, so particularly itself, that—well really, I *must* show you! . . . There!" Or the writer explains, "Just so and just so it happened, or might happen, and thus the heart shook, and thus . . ." And suddenly, deliciously, with them you see and feel.

Art is not a criticism of Life. There *is* a side of it that makes problems clear, throws light on the complexity of modern life, assists one to understand. It is a function much dwelt on nowadays. A section of modern drama is praised for explaining religion, or the relation of the sexes, or of Capital and Labour. It is incidental. Discussion is merely one of the means, not the end, of literary art. You are in the midst of insoluble problems of temperance reform and education and organization. The artist, as artist, is not concerned. He leads you away by the hand and, Mamillius-like, begins his tale: "There was a man—dwelt by a churchyard"—it is purely irrelevant.

But how important these intimate irrelevances are! I hold the view most fervently. If not this paper would be found inexcusable—quite inexcusable. Yet I must apologize to those who hold it a waste of time to consider anything for the moment but material social reform. With all my soul I'm with them. I feel deeply with Morris when he cries out about "filling up this terrible gap between riches and poverty. Doubtless many things will go to filling it up, and if Art must be one of those things, let it go. (What business have we with Art at all unless we can share it?) I am not afraid but that Art will rise from the Dead, whatever else lies there". And if it were a choice between keeping the Arts and establishing a high National Minimum, I would not hesitate a moment. I hate the *dilettante* and unimaginative hypocrisy that would. But things don't happen that way. We have forsworn Revolution for a jog-trot along Social Reform, and there is plenty of time to take things with us on the way—Art above all. The tradition of art-work and artists is worth keeping—the sort of tradition, I mean, that links Milton and Keats and Francis Thompson. It is a jumping ground, not a clog. The heritage is valuable. Art, if it cannot make men much better as means, can make them very good as ends. To most people it can give something. To some it can give the highest and supremest part of their lives. It multiplies the value of the life we are trying to organize to have. Not only for the moments when we hear or read or see the Arts do we prize them, though these would be hard to know the full worth of. But when the tree or the wall or the situation meets us in real life, they find profounder hosts. In the transience and hurry Art opens out every way on to the Eternal Ends.

* * * * *

Democracy and the Arts! This paper, like all good papers, has given its first half to saying what it's going to be about. Like all good papers it had better give most of its second half to saying why it is about it.

Partly because, as I have said, we are on the way to extinguish artists by destroying the systems which enabled them to live. Only the most fanatical and the most immediately popular could survive—by no means the best types. But in any case other systems have been irregular and bad—most of all the present one. We can do something far better. Also, we *must* realize that in a thousand ways new conditions and vast possibilities are round us and ahead. The circumstances of modern life offer new temptations and new dangers to the artist. Enormous potential art publics grow slowly before our eyes. And both they and the artist are increasingly helpless before the blind amoral profit-hunger of the commercial. We must not be unprepared for the effects these dark multitudes will have on the Arts.

The question of the Public of the future requires consideration, though it is not the central point of this paper. We want it large and varied. A culture sustained by an infinitesimal group of the infinitely elect will not be possible or desirable. Though, indeed, there are, and increasingly will be, many groups each thinking itself to be such: and a good thing too, so long as the conditions of modern life keep the groups from getting too isolated and stagnant. We need not complain if the Public only means a mass of little publics. It would be a good thing if the whole artistic public of England twenty years hence would delight in Gauguin. We shall be content if half a million worship the Impressionists, and half a million adore the Post-Impressionists. It may be one of the conditions of life. It is especially one of the things we must fearlessly accustom ourselves to, the growth of diverse circles and publics, to whom local or special kinds of poets and painters will appeal. From such artists the greater, and more widely reaching, will roughly emerge, spreading to other circles, more distant ears and eyes. It used to be, in a general way, true to say of a great author—of Dryden or Johnson or Pope—that all England read them—all England that read any literature. That time has utterly gone—it is not realized how irrevocably that time has gone. There are twenty millions who read in England today, millions of them reading literature. The numbers of a potential literary public increase enormously year by year. No one man, except one or two classics, can touch more than a fraction. This change in the old conditions, this breaking up of unity, this multitude of opening minds, may bring perplexity and apparent confusion of standards; but also (I say it soberly) the chance of vast, unimaginable, unceasing additions to the glory of the literature of England.

There are two other points, points on which many go wrong when they contemplate the present and future publics for the Arts. There is the mistake of the man who says, "When Everyman has reached a decent amount of leisure and education, the whole community will foster and patronize and delight in the Arts". An inspection of the class that has had leisure and education does not justify this opinion. It may be objected that public school education is not good. That is true. But it will be a long time before you can ensure the whole nation getting a considerably better education than the modern public school and university one. And even then I do not suppose more than a small part of the nation will ever be much interested in the Arts, though it is easy to imagine a state of things coming to pass where perhaps most people will pretend to be. But such things are beyond our vista. The first generation of universal education has not given us a nation of art-lovers. Nor will the second, nor the third. We must face the problem on the assumption that public demand isn't going to settle much of it for us for a long while yet.

And then there's the idea that the lower classes, the people who are entering into the circle of the educated, are coarsely devoid of taste, likely to swamp—swamping—the whole of culture in un-distinguished, raucous, stumpy arts that know no tradition. If the washy, dull, dead upper-class brains this idea haunts were its only home we could leave it. But it lurks in the Victorian shadows and dusty corners of finer types of mind. Ideas in other parts of this paper may help to kill it, I hope. I would say one or two things about it here. In the first place, it is not relevant that the newly encivilized and educated classes should not be able to leap at once to the superb heights to which we have toiled through so many generations. It is the future—their future fineness—we work for. It is only natural that the taste of the lower classes should be at present infinitely worse than ours. The amazing thing is that it is probably rather better. It is true many Trades Unionists do not read

Milton. Nor do many University men. But take the best of each. Compare the literary criticism of the *Labour Leader* with that of the *Saturday Review*. It is, I assure you, enormously better, enormously readier to recognize good new literature. Think of the working-class support of Miss Horniman's Repertory Theatre in Manchester. Compare the fate of the progeny of middle- and upper-class intellectualism, Mr. Frohman's Repertory Theatre, and the Vedrenne-Barker company, and Mr. Herbert Trench's dream. Compare the style of the *Cambridge History of English Literature* with that of Mr. Arnold Bennett's handbook on the subject. They are separated—how can I express the difference?—more widely than Hell and Heaven. The gulf that parts them is the greatest gulf there is, the one which divides the dead from the living. Put, finally—for we must stop this sometime—put the *Spectator* beside the *Clarion* for pure literary merit. I do not wish to decry the *Spectator*. In common with many other Socialists I have written in it. But—on the honour of an enthusiast for literature—the *Clarion* wins all the way. Those who have determined to make the State we live in, and are forming for the future, as fine as possible, must be very careful to oppose the force of primness in this matter. Unnecessarily to divide the traditions we have got from the new life of the time, to assist in divorcing good taste from popular literature, is to rob and weaken both. Those whose test of painting is perspective, whose test of literature is the absence of split infinitives, cry

"Vulgarity!" and "Bad Grammar!" They are the epithets corpses fling at the quick, dead languages at living. Accept them and pass on. They do not matter. More, they are praise.

I have met a group of young poets in London. Some of them are in money extremely poor. They talk Cockney. And they write—some are good, others bad—as they talk. That is to say, their poems give fullest value when pronounced as they thought and felt them. They allow for *ow* being *aow*. Their love-poems begin (I invent) "If yew wd come agin to me". That is healthy. That way is life. In them is more hope—and more fulfilment—than in the old-world passion and mellifluous despair of any gentle-man's or lady's poetry.

To sum up, the influence of Democracy on the Arts from this point of view—the Public—need not be bad. To show that it is good, and to make it better, it is most importantly our duty to welcome and aid all the new and wider movements that come with the growth of Democracy and the rise of new genera-tions. I say new generations, for we are old-fashioned I find, in danger of being out of touch, we whose life is divided between university, a few similar people in London, and the country rectories that are our homes. And it is even more important when we see the idols we most worship attacked and crumb-bling, to acquiesce, to accept where we cannot under-stand, to endure the boots and accent of the unrefined in the sanctuary, for the sake of the new Gods that follow. It will be very difficult.

But the subject I am most concerned with now is, as I said at the beginning, that of the Artist himself, how we are to make certain of his turning up. It would be more amusing than profitable to go into the economic status of the Artist in past times, a study that has not been sufficiently worked out. At least notice that no past age can jeer at us and go unscathed. Take literature. To each generation of the last century we can reply with John Clare and James Thomson and Francis Thompson. Ask those of the great age of letters, the eighteenth century, what they did with Chatterton, who might have been the greatest of them all. Consider Michael Drayton, and a dozen more of the Elizabethans. The truth is that no system has worked well for long. With painters I believe the guild system did for a time. The State in Athens, founded, we are told, on popular good taste, out-rivalled the great courts of Syracuse and elsewhere. Our problems are different from theirs; our machinery cannot be so simple. Patronage is often loosely praised, held up to us as the golden age for artists. It is grossly over-estimated. Once or twice it has worked: Italy will witness. And the conception of musicians, poets and painters, healthy and wealthy, crowding round a prince of perfect taste, perfect appearance, and immense generosity, is delightful. But who will honestly hope our millionaires will fill their distinguished places? And it was an untrust-worthy transient business. It only works with a small rich court of highly cultured people. Patronage, to be of great use, must endow the artist thoroughly.

The ordinary system of incomplete endowment and jobbery and such things as payment for dedications, was a ramshackle affair. You see it at work in Elizabethan times, when most of the best writers lost all their shame (which doesn't much matter) and half their vitality (which does) in cadging and touting. They were in continual poverty and debt, and driven to hackwork. Few dramatists could make as much as the equivalent of £200 a year. Jobbing was all right when it could be invoked and if it jobbed the man into a sinecure. Often, as with Spenser, it didn't. So we have lost half the *Faery Queen* (oh, *I* shouldn't care if we'd lost it all. It's the principle of the thing). It has been the same since. It is impossible to know how much more Milton and Marvell would have given us if they had had money enough to live on. If anything at all, the loss is enormous. If Dryden and Addison had not had to sell themselves to politics, our literature could only have gained.

Only in a few cases and in a few kinds of literature have writers been able to make a living. Even lately and with the most popular this is true. Tennyson did not make enough to live on till he was middle-aged. He had to put off his marriage eleven years. Tom Hood, a great writer, both comic and serious, was, artistically, ruined by the continuous flood of jokes he had to pour forth all his life. And, in the waste of the past centuries, you must not only count the cases of starvation or over-production, nor even the artistic potentialities sown here and there in the undistinguished mass of the people, which have perished unconscious in that blindest oblivion—the mute inglorious Miltons of the village and slum Beethovens—but also the many who have had the chance of an artist's career that would have produced good, and have not thought the risk worth while. Alfred Tennyson died, but was not born, the only poet in that family.

And nowadays : it is worth considering what we do, or rather what Fate does, now, to enable artists to produce works of art. It is terrifying, when you examine the matter, to find how many of them live on unearned, presumably inherited, capital. As there are comparatively few people who can do this, a million or two, and as we are going to reduce the number, it is an alarming outlook. The only creative artistic profession you have much chance of making a living at, fairly soon, is that of a dramatist. I suppose it is almost inconceivable that a creative musician can live by composing till he has passed thirty ; few then. It is in the process of making a public that the modern artist has to have extraneous financial support or go under. (There are various ways of going under. Mr. Somerset Maugham and Mr. Hall Caine chose one way, the better. Rimbaud, who went East and was last heard of driving a caravan in Arabia,[1] another. Chatterton a third.) The painter's only hope is to paint the portraits of the extremely rich and extremely undistinguished. It is not always

[1] Brooke is here at fault. Rimbaud, after travelling in Abyssinia, died in hospital at Marseilles.

open, nor always attractive, to him to take the revenge Sargent sometimes takes. In future, perhaps, we'll have our big painters painting the great, not the rich.

Poetry is even worse off than the other arts. Even Mr. Rudyard Kipling could not live on his poetry. Very few poets, perhaps one or two in five years, sell 1000 copies of a volume. If they do, and if they find a very generous publisher, and if they charge 5s. for their volume (an absurdly high price) they get £25! An experienced publisher's reader tells me no one in England makes £50 a year by poetry—except perhaps Mr. Kipling and Mr. A. Noyes. Fiction's far better: but you can't live by writing good fiction —so writers of good fiction inform me. Henry James can *now*, no doubt, at sixty. He could not if he were thirty.

What then, as we grow more democratic and more people have to work for their living, since the noblest work of all does not produce a livelihood, are we to do? To make a great creative artist is beyond the power of eugenist or schoolmaster. All we can hope to do is to spot them when they come, and enable them to realize their genius. We have laid down one axiom—the artist is to be free from other work. If you won't do that, at any rate let the other work be as disgusting as possible. An artist will do better art-work in intervals if his livelihood is got by cleaning sewers than if he takes up some more fascinating occupation, like teaching or critical work. But if we're going to do away with the very

D

clumsy and inefficient machinery of patrons (who don't work at all now) and inherited capital, we, the community, must endow the artist. This has often enough been put forward as a necessary part of some Utopian—probably strongly Collectivist—State, the sort of State the year 2050 may see. I submit that it is a thing that should be begun now. It should go on concurrently with taxation; be a financially minor, but actually important, part of the annual Budget. It is absurd to wait till the Death Duties have done their work, to begin remedying the bad effects of it. With scholarships, of course, a little is done this way; but very little and very clumsily and very unconsciously. This evening I want to suggest a few ideas about endowment. If people accept the general theory, a detailed plan would not be hard to elaborate. It is the sort of idea that must be accepted generally as commonsense, not a startling novelty, and must be part of the ordinary background of people's minds. Fix your eye firmly on what we want to do, to endow the great creative artists. Now it must obviously be endowment for ever. It is no use paying a man to learn the intricacies of musical composition for seven or eight years and then leaving him stranded. It is just the greatest who would suffer. Verdi might come out of it all right : not Wagner. Nor can we have anyone dictating to the artists how they must work, on pain of having their scholarships taken away. A system so brilliantly efficacious with undergraduates and schoolboys would not work in this case. Nor, of course, could questions of morality enter. And the endowment must not be removed if the artist becomes popular enough to earn a living without it. We don't want to prolong the present condition by which, if an artist strikes a vein which is popular, he is economically bound to continue in it for the rest of his life. By that, Shakespeare, being successful with histories, daren't proceed to *As You Like It*, or, having "scored a success" in comedy, can't go on to *Hamlet*. No, the endowment must be unconditioned, even, I suggest, as regards production. We might perhaps insist on one picture, book, or piece of music in ten years. Nothing more stringent. The only debatable point seems to me to be the forbidding of other trades. We *might* forbid them to earn money by doing quite different work to any large extent. No doubt the Government will begin that way. I expect it's not worth doing, though. There are a lot of details, like the increase of endowment if the artist married. The Eugenics Society would see we got that.

The point where most people profess to find the greatest difficulty is in the machinery for selecting people for endowment. "The State", they say, "is always stupid about Art". Also "a Committee always compromises". They talk of "officialdom". As every Socialist knows, these silly generalizations are always being flung in to cloak muddled thinking. To begin with, the State hasn't tried anything of this kind. It has only muddled feebly with Art here and there. To argue from that is like bringing up the bad management of occasional railways by individualist governments as an argument against the considered socialization of monopolies. In any case, State activity is not uniformly stupid. The Royal Academy perhaps is bad. The National Gallery is good. So, on the whole, is the Civil List—as far as it goes. The chief faults in these two departments are those of meanness. We can remedy that if we want to.

As far as efficiency of endowment goes, any modern Cabinet Minister with a few hundred thousand a year to spend and the advice of a couple of literary journalists would be more successful, and infinitely less wasteful, than the present system of capital. But that is a low standard. And the one-man method is not the best. A committee is obvious. It is a system that fulfills its purpose very well, for example, in electing to college fellowships, especially where the number of fellowships is large. For notice, the ordinary objections to a committee on an æsthetic subject apply only when it is to choose some single object. A committee of artists met to select one from one thousand designs, say for a bridge across the Thames, will compromise and not choose the most beautiful. But if the Supreme and Omniscient Art Critic required them to pick the ten most beautiful, and gave them one hundred shots, they would probably succeed. And that is what we want. Take the endowment of pure creative literature. I conceive of a committee of, say, thirty. It could and should be constituted in many different ways, by nomination by the Crown, by, perhaps, the Universities, by various official and semi-official bodies such as the

Society of Authors, and in other ways—the more irregular the better. You'd get a few stuffy people, no doubt; you'd also get a few creative artists, Thomas Hardy and Yeats, and critics like Professor Sir Walter Raleigh and Mr. Gosse. They would have outer circles of advisers and suggesters. It seems to me certain that, if such a Committee had to choose one hundred writers of poetry to endow, and voted on some system of proportional representation, in such a way that two or three, or even one, who was keen enough, could make certain of a candidate, they would sweep in almost every writer who could possibly turn out to be any good. Remember, it is people like these who have always been the first to recognize genius. Think how Tennyson or James Thomson or Yeats or Meredith were discovered. Think, from the other side, of the work Henley and Ben Jonson did.

It may be objected that we should waste a lot in endowing failures, ten of them perhaps for every one even moderate success. Certainly. It is an integral part of the scheme. The choice is between endowing twenty Tuppers to one Byron—and endowing neither; and the present system, which consists in endowing twenty thousand Tuppers and one Byron, *and*—for that might be worth while—very effectually disendowing and spoiling twenty million Tuppers—and who dare say how many Byrons among them?

Indeed, I'd have you notice that the kind of failures we endow are likely to be useful to our purpose. There is frequently among artists of all kinds generosity that seems extraordinary in a commercial age. The example of French painters is a notable one. And there are several cases today in literature, where good writers of some genius have been helped with money, advice and advertisement, most freely and solely for their genius' sake, by smaller writers of more fortunate lot—just the kind who would have been endowed on their early promise, and would not have accomplished anything great.

That is all to the good. For we must insist on the need for as many channels as possible through which the Arts may be subsidized. Each additional channel may mean fresh artists who would have escaped our notice otherwise; and each helps to provide for fresh, unexpected developments.

Besides the central State endowments it would be a good thing to have more local and special ones. If the numerous universities of Great Britain could be given money to endow creative artistic work, it would be excellent. At present they only endow critical work and knowledge. They would be able to do the other, too, quite admirably. Municipalities also might be encouraged to take steps in that direction. The more progressive of them are ready enough to be the first, driven by those motives of honourable rivalry which already have so finely influenced some of our great cities and districts. With the present growth of local pride, and of universities in large centres, and with the system of County Council scholarships, it should be easy to encourage local endowment of Art, with desirable results of variety and thoroughness. I can imagine Manchester and others being keen enough to get the credit of connexion with the next great painter or dramatist.

This local connexion may be increased and improved incidentally by a plan that has been suggested, by which the local or national authority endowing might receive, under conditions, a share in, or the whole of, the copyright of an endowed artist's work after his death. This applies only, apparently, to music and books. But the lines on which it may be extended to pictures can be seen if you consider the admirable proposal that a percentage of the *increase* in value of a picture should go to the artist or his heirs every time it is sold. This copyright business may allay the fears of the parsimonious, for obviously the State would begin to *gain* by the endowment of Art in a generation. Still it is very important. The cost of endowing Art in England is absurdly small. Suppose you give artists an average of £500 a year—and I personally think *half* that is all that is necessary. Endow for life two hundred musicians, two hundred painters and sculptors, two hundred poets, and three hundred other creative literary men, keeping one hundred endowments for special richness in one section or unclassified creative artistic genius, you would spend half a million a year. Half a million! I need not tell students of modern budgets what a drop that is. If anyone wants to realize its insignificance let him consider modern expenditure on armaments. Half a million to secure the Arts in England! (I appeal to my friends the

politicians in this Society to see that this is done!)
If there's any politician present there's his chance!

* * * * *

Each Art has different conditions and demands
different treatment. I am afraid I have considered too
much the conditions of Literature. But the principles
of endowment apply throughout in music and painting. The system of scholarships from County Council
and other schools is good enough, but must be
continually increased. We want to drain the nation.
More scholarships should come both through the
County Councils and at the various Academies and
Colleges of Music and Art, which, conditionally,
could be State-aided. They must be sufficient in
amount and period. People should be able to travel
and study on them.

(If anyone wants to know how well, even now,
such scholarships can be applied, he can examine
the L.C.C. Art scholarships. To be sure they don't
lead to dead Official Art, ask anyone at the Slade
School of Art, which is not generally thought to be
over-academic. He will tell you of the extraordinarily
good scholars they get from the L.C.C. You will
learn of the Michael Angelo of the twentieth century,
as a youth is named who has been discovered in the
back streets of London, and can draw better than any
upper-class rival. It is the right process. I'm told by
people at the Slade that the holders of L.C.C. scholarships are some of the best people there. And that

they should be sent or be able to go to the Slade shows that these municipal bodies wouldn't encourage only dead official art.)

I will not worry about more details. I only want to insist that endowment is the only thing for us to do, and is immediately necessary. In considering such a scheme certain requirements must be kept in mind as a guide. The artist must be able to devote himself to his work. He must be left to himself as much as possible. He should have, I think, an economic spur to production and popularity, the chance, that is, of greater wealth if his work catches on. And endowment should be of as various kinds as possible.

And besides all these more or less official forces at work, we must see that there are private ones. More and more as the public for the Arts grows wider shall we find private societies and groups in immense variety helping our work. This may take the form of endowment, group-patronage, an excellent thing, already less rare than is generally known. It requires a genuine and rather beautiful faith in an artist's work and future for large numbers of his friends to sacrifice something in order that he may be able to realize his fate unhindered. But more usually these societies will be bands of consumers, of purchasers, acting together to be more effective, combining to finance the production of new plays or music, or to buy pictures and statues. I do not refer to such bodies as the National Art Collections Fund or the Friends of the Fitzwilliam Museum. Their work is excellent. But it only indirectly affects the living artist. No activity of theirs would have saved Monticelli or Epstein or Van Gogh or Clare or Nerval from the hindrances and degradation of poverty. I mean rather an extension and multiplication of the Contemporary Art Society, which buys modern pictures before they have become old masters. It will be private bodies, formed in such ways, that will come to the rescue, perhaps, when the great event happens for which our prayers go up night and day, and a great writer or painter or composer appears, so monstrously blasphemous or indecent that the most hardened Municipality or University or member of the National Endowment Committee will have nothing to do with him.

There is, perhaps, one more aspect of Democracy and the Arts besides the Public and the Artist, which can be mentioned. It is one on which a whole book might throw light—two pages are useless. It is the question of what fools call the æsthetic aspirations of the community, and journalists call an atmosphere, and hard clear thinkers vow non-existent, and wise men know to be an attitude of mind. Is there anything more we can do about the artistic atmosphere in this Democracy? Is it possible to ensure that artist and critic will be living, eager about new productions and experiments, believing in their arts? What should our own attitude of mind be?

There is nothing, I suppose, to be *done*, except indirectly by smashing smugness and propriety, and encouraging enthusiasm rather than criticism in the world. All one can do is to turn out a great many artists and critics (real critics). This sort of thing is a matter of tradition largely. You get a whole lot of people, a class or a town or circle, falling naturally into the belief that Art is worth while and means a lot to them. They mostly lie. But they are necessary. Remember that, when a lot of idiots yearn to you about the Irish plays. *They* are the condition of J. M. Synge. Concerts, we hear, are hard enough to get up in Cambridge. If only those who cared for the music went they would be impossible. The Arts are built up on a crowd of prattlers, *dilettanti*, wits and pseudo-cultured. It is worth while.

But there is one thing we can do. To give vitality to the Arts it is necessary to direct a large proportion of our interest to contemporary art. The need for this is not fully recognized, especially in that half-cultivated class *we* belong to. There are two points about it I should like to mention. One is the obvious one that has already come out. It is our *duty* to be interested in contemporary art for the artist's sake, first that he may live, second that he may turn out better stuff. All your praise of Shakespeare will not turn him to his too neglected task of "blotting" at any rate *some* lines : nor will Leonardo ever complete his head of Christ. But the living, them you can stir or warm and enable to work, and work at their best. Do you think this unnecessary, slightly insulting? Is anyone muttering, "But we *are* modern and up-to-date. Nietzsche is our Bible. Van Gogh our idol. We drink in the lessons of Meredith and Ibsen and Swinburne and Tolstoy ! . . . Dostoieffsky and Tour-

genieff. . . ." They are dead, my friends, all dead.
Beware, for the generations slip imperceptibly into
one another, and it is so much easier to accept standards that are prepared for you. Beware of the dead.

But it is not only a question of duty to living artists
—a sufficiently dreary appeal. So much sentimentality
has been talked about the immortality of Art that
it is a *heresy* that I now suggest to you. To open eyes
the nature of Art forbids this immortality. If you
write a poem on Tuesday it begins to die on Wednes-
day. Some take longer dying than others. That is all.
Anyhow a few thousand years will finish off the
Parthenon Marbles, and Shakespeare will not outlive
half a dozen more civilizations. But time has a
quicker, quieter way than that. Necessary to Art is
the recipient, and he must change. No man alive can
read Shakespeare quite as Shakespeare meant it.
The subtle shades of words have changed. The
Elizabethans' common words seem strange to us.
And we can never recapture the fine thrill of sur-
prise they had at words that were delightful fresh
inventions of theirs—words like *prejudice*. There is
something in almost all Art that only a contemporary
can get—only one who shares with the artist the
general feeling for ideas and thoughts and outlook
of the time. *That* is the great reason for interest in
the art of one's own time. Think of what we *do* feel
and value. Take—I pick almost at random—Henry
James's last volume of stories, and, most delightful
in the most delightful of them,[1] the phrase, "She just

[1] "A Round of Visits" in *The Finer Grain*, 1910.

charmingly hunched her eyes at him". Thirty years
hence and for ever after, will they be able to get just
what we get from that, in meaning and intonation,
the caress of the adverb, the exact shade of comedy in
the verb, the curve of the sentence?

*   *   *   *   *

There is much to be said. But it is late, and each can
say it for himself, if only he'll do what people
romantically never will do, for all my persuasion—
only connect Art and Democracy. Upper-class young
people who live on money they don't earn and
dabble with painting or writing (I am one) are
always, and so finely, a little too *temperamentvoll* to
be interested in "politics". It's much easier and much
splendider to assume that social organization or disor-
ganization has no effect on people—on artists at least:
to fly off with some splashing war-cry that "Art will
out", that "The True Artist (wonderful abstraction!)
is only Improved by Poverty". The wonderful old-
world romanticism of it all! The fineness, even, when
it's done by poor people! It's only when it's carelessly
flung out by people who *have* an assured unearned
few hundreds a year, that the sentiment may ring a
little discordant, taste a trifle unwholesome, something like Lord Rosebery's, to the over-sensitive
palate. You feel that if the misty splendour of these
artists turned perspicuous, it would for a second
reveal them leaning after all against an ordinary wall,
in an attitude that's exactly between the ever so

slightly silly and the ever so slightly something worse.
Like the lovers at the end of the modern poem:

> Flamingly, flamingly good as ends,
> Heart of my heart, are dividends.

And against them stand the politicians, who are only
occupied with social and political changes: who also,
less gloriously, leave Art to take care of itself. Now
more than ever. "Politics", I heard two old clergy-
men in Oxford say, on a tram last July, "are no
laughing matter nowadays". Those who never found
them a laughing matter will be full these days of
vaster questions than endowing artists. Their hearts
thrill with great cries—Home Rule—Insurance—
Peace. In such a mood "Democracy" is only a long
word, a mouthful, a battle-cry, a sound that evokes
tumultuous applause and right voting: or perhaps an
emotional dim ideal. Regard it as a present process.
The word should picture *us*, with our habits of feeling
and thought, and, more particularly, thousands and
millions of wakening minds everywhere. More than
a million Trades Unionists, a million belonging to
P.S.A. Brotherhoods, bodies with an outlook and
importance we haven't dimly begun to grasp, the
W.E.A., the Adult Schools—these and many more
are spreading, further than ever our narrow conceits
carry, fresh enthusiasms and loyalties and intellectual
keenness. These, and we, and the traditions and
institutions of the land, and the infinite entanglement
of will and instinct and fate, individual and collective,
are bound together weaving the future. It is possible
and desirable to guard and aid the Arts as Democracy

grows. But it must be by a conscious effort, by not being afraid of new things, by helping to build up an atmosphere and tradition of honour for the Arts, by living in the present as well as in the past, and especially, and more easily because more tangibly, by endowing artists, we can do this. Like the rest of the great adventure of Democracy it is a superb, an exhilarating chance. We, rotund and comfortable, are willy-nilly rolling out on the most amazing expedition. There's but one danger, one misconception more I would point out. Two years ago I heard a lecture on Social Reform and the Drama, delivered by a great living critic, a keen, able, solemn, whiskered, well-meaning man, Mr. William Archer. His theory was that Art depends for its subject-matter (a) on people having so much money and so much leisure as to be able to get into scrapes; (b) on social injustice and evil laws which lead to misery. Conclusion: successful social reform on democratic lines means the end of Art. He was, it is unnecessary to say, in earnest. It is a theory that has crept into too many minds. It is the ultimate disloyalty—not to Democracy, but to Art. We need not point out that all the poets and dramatists and half the painters have found their subject matter in the past. Nor need we bring up those artists from Whitman to Meunier who have begun to invade the vast new provinces now opening to them. We shall—rather we *will*—find that the old unchanging ground for the artist stands fast, the emotions of the individual human heart. Imagination will only grow profounder, passions and terrors will come in stranger shapes. Tragedy and Comedy will not leave the world while two things stay in it, the last two that Civilization will cure us of, Death and Fools. In new shapes Hamlet and Othello and Macbeth will move among us, as they do today. Though we perfect the marriage laws it will still be possible to fall in love with the wrong person or with two people; and still painful. Still, while Democracy grows, down the ages we may have the figure of a critic, an elderly man, explaining to a group of young people that the stuff of Art is being ruled out of life, black-whiskered and perplexed and in earnest—slightly resembling Matthew Arnold, a recurrent figure of most excellent comic value.